A STEP-BY-STEP GUIDE FOR THE ASPIRING COMICS ARTIST

DRAW COMICS

A STEP-BY-STEP GUIDE FOR THE ASPIRING COMICS ARTIST

TONY TALLARICO

Mud Puddle Books

NEW YORK

Draw Comics
A Step-by-Step Guide for the Aspiring Comics Artist
By Tony Tallarico

© 1995 by Tony Tallarico

This edition published in 2006 by
Mud Puddle Books, Inc.
54 W. 21st Street
Suite 601
New York, NY 10010
info@mudpuddlebooks.com

ISBN: 978-1-60311-039-6

Originally published as
Drawing and Cartooning Comics
The Berkeley Publishing Company.
New York

Printed and bound in China

CONTENTS

THIS ENTIRE BOOK — LIKE MOST COMICS — WAS HAND LETTERED.
THIS IS HOW TO DO IT —

CONSTRUCTION

THE ANATOMY OF LETTERING ....

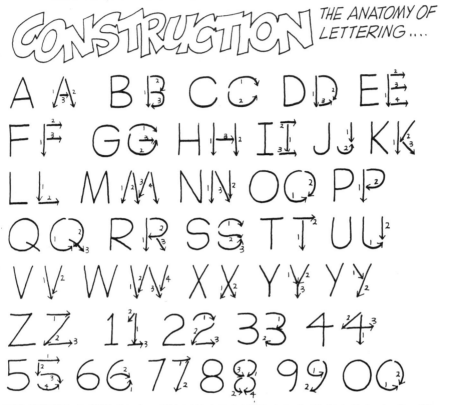

THE FIRST STEP IN ACTUALLY LETTERING A BALLOON IS TO
ROUGHLY LAY OUT THE LETTERING IN PENCIL. NEXT PLACE PENCIL
GUIDE LINES (3/16" FOR LTG., 1/8" SPACE BETWEEN LINES). THEN TIGHTEN UP THE
PENCIL LETTERING (IN PENCIL), THEN INK. (YOU CAN ELIMINATE THE
TIGHTENING UP IN PENCIL ONCE YOU'VE BECOME PROFICIENT IN
LETTERING.) THE LAST STEP IS TO PLACE THE BALLOON.

ROUGH PENCIL   *GUIDE LINES AND TIGHTEN-UP*   *INK LETTERING AND BALLOON*

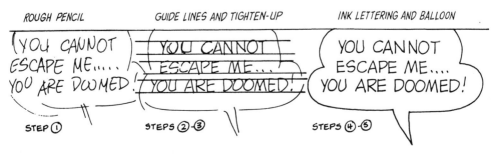

STEP ①   STEPS ②-③   STEPS ④-⑤

⑧

 **SPACING** (ALL LETTERING WAS DONE USING A "B-6" PEN WITH INDIA INK OR A "FLAIR" MARKING PEN.)

THE GREATEST AMOUNT OF SPACE BETWEEN LETTERS IS WHEN YOU HAVE 2 STRAIGHT LINE LETTERS NEXT TO EACH OTHER AS IN THE CASE OF THE WORD

HIE

THE NEXT LEAST AMOUNT IS WHEN AN OPEN LETTER IS NEXT TO A STRAIGHT ONE...

THE

THE LEAST AMOUNT OF SPACE IS WHEN 2 OPEN LETTERS ARE NEXT TO EACH OTHER...

CAPTAIN

LOGOS – THE **FUN** PART OF LETTERING!

USE THE SAME STEPS AS YOU WOULD TO DO BASIC LETTERING –

ACTION!

ACTION!

ACTION!

① DRAW GUIDE LINES AND ROUGH OUT WORD.

② CONSTRUCT THE LETTERS.

③ FINISHED LETTERING.

ILLUSTRATE THE MOOD –

EASY JAZZY

SHADE

ALWAYS PLAN AHEAD

SERGEANT SKETCH

THE PENCIL IS MIGHTIER THAN THE SWORD!

THIS IS A SIMPLE OUTLINE DRAWING WITH DETAILS — BUT WITHOUT BLACK AREAS. TURN THE PAGE TO FIND OUT HOW TO ADD SHADOWS AND DEPTH TO THIS PICTURE.

ALL DRAWINGS ARE BASED ON BASIC SHAPES.
ALWAYS DRAW THE FIRST THREE STEPS LIGHTLY IN PENCIL.
NEVER ADD DETAILS TO YOUR DRAWING UNTIL YOU HAVE
COMPLETED DRAWING AND ARE SATISFIED WITH THE BASIC SHAPES.

LIGHTING

SIMPLE SIDE LIGHTING.

LIGHT SOURCE

SIDE LIGHTING WITH SHADOWS.

LIGHT SOURCE

LIGHT SOURCE OVERHEAD LIGHT SOURCE.

LIGHT SOURCE

FRONT LIGHT SOURCE

AS YOU CAN SEE — THE SAME DRAWING CAN BE GIVEN VARIOUS LOOKS BY CHANGING THE SOURCE OF LIGHTING.

BACK
LIGHTING.

LIGHT
SOURCE

THIS EFFECT
WAS ACHIEVED
BY DRAWING
ALL THE LINES
TO ONE POINT
(SEE LEFT HAND).

THE SAME BASIC DRAWING
ONLY WITHOUT A LIGHT
SOURCE. INSTEAD, BLACK
AREAS ARE USED AS
LOCAL COLOR.

READY FOR ACTION

MAKE YOUR OWN
LIGHTING SOURCE
FOR THIS
FIGURE.

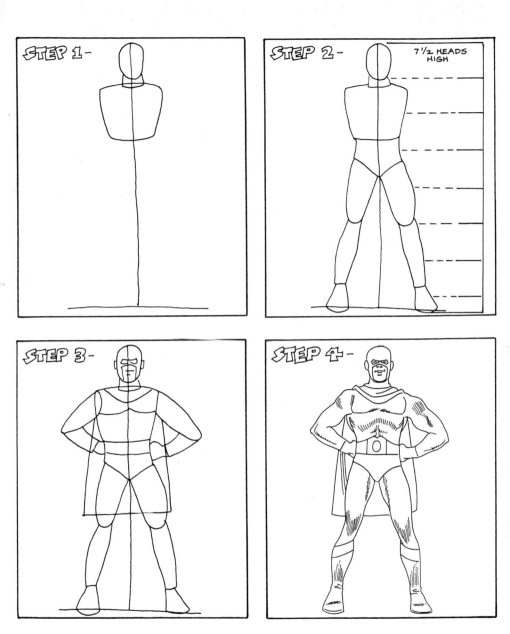

STEP 1 –

STEP 2 – 7 1/2 HEADS HIGH

STEP 3 –

STEP 4 –

AFTER USING THE BASIC SHAPES OF THE FIGURE, YOU CAN CREATE YOUR OWN COSTUME FOR THIS HERO.

A CAPED HERO

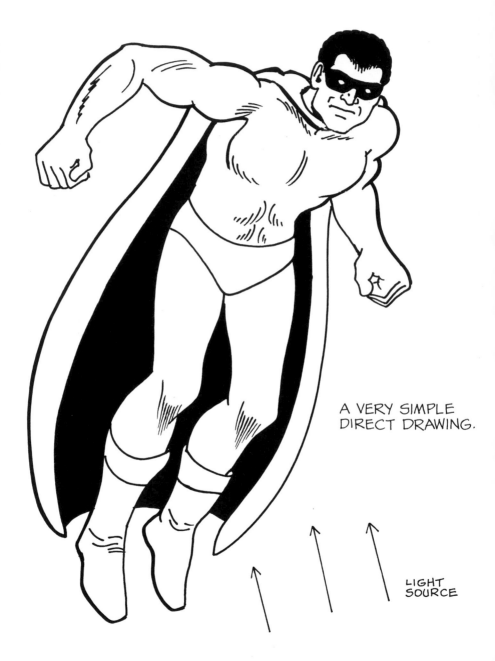

A VERY SIMPLE
DIRECT DRAWING.

LIGHT
SOURCE

COMPLETE THE BASIC SHAPES OF THE ARMS BEFORE
DRAWING THE CAPE SHAPE LIGHTLY IN PENCIL.

SPEED QUEEN

SIMPLE LIGHTING AND LOCAL COLOR HAVE BEEN USED. TRY THIS WITH A DIFFERENT LIGHT SOURCE.

THIS IS AN OPPORTUNITY TO COMBINE LETTERING WITH ART.

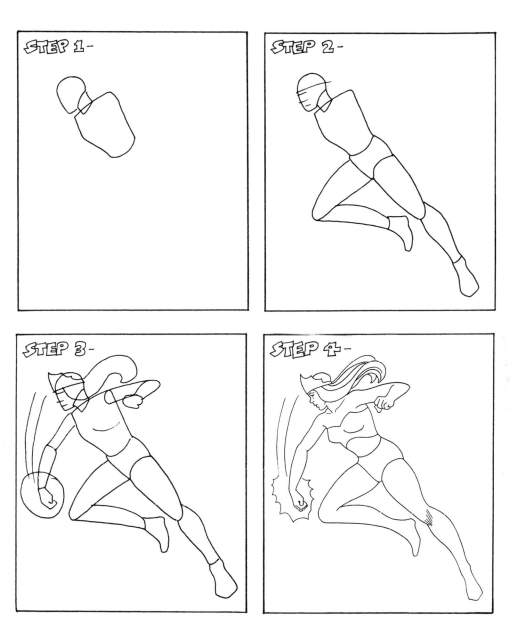

AS SIMPLE AS THIS ACTION FIGURE APPEARS, YOU MUST BUILD ON THE BASIC SHAPES BEFORE YOU ADD DETAILS.

ANY SHADOW CAN BE MADE SOFTER BY *FEATHERING* THE SIDE THAT FACES THE LIGHT SOURCE.

LIGHT SOURCE

SPEED LINES HAVE BEEN USED TO SHOW DIRECTION AND SPEED.

JUST A SUGGESTION OF A GROUND LINE ESTABLISHES THAT SHE IS FLYING.

THIS FIGURE IS OVER EIGHT HEADS HIGH.

MS. HEROINE

A SIMPLE NIGHT SKY AND CITY LANDSCAPE ADD
DIMENSION TO THE FIGURE.

THE FLOW OF THE CAPE SHOWS THAT THE FIGURE'S ACTION
IS IN A DOWN DIRECTION.

EVIL DOME-HEAD

A BAD GUY THAT MAKES A
MESS OF BRICK WALLS.
HE ALSO NEEDS A SHAVE.

THE ONLY SOLID BLACK
AREA IS ON THE MASK.
ALL OTHER SHADOWS WERE DRAWN
USING SHORT PEN STROKES.

DON'T BE AFRAID TO DRAW THROUGH OR TO ERASE
IN THE FIRST THREE STEPS.

CHECKERS

ALL SHADOWS WERE DRAWN BY USING SHORT PEN STROKES GOING IN THE SAME DIRECTION.

ADD A FEW CLOUDS TO ESTABLISH THAT HE IS FLYING IN THE SKY.

THE HANDS ARE LARGER THAN HIS FACE BECAUSE
THEY ARE THE CLOSEST THINGS TO THE VIEWER.

LEAPING LINDA

THE FLAMES BELOW
ACT AS THE LIGHT SOURCE.

STEP 1-

STEP 2-

STEP 3-

STEP 4-

HER FOOT MEASURES LARGER THAN HER HEAD BECAUSE IT IS
THE PART OF HER BODY THAT IS CLOSEST TO THE
VIEWER.

CRIME FIGHTER

IN HIS SPARE TIME
HE LOOKS AS IF HE
PLAYS BASS IN A
HEAVY METAL BAND.

BE SURE YOUR BASIC SHAPES ARE CORRECT BEFORE
COMPLETING YOUR DRAWING IN STEP FOUR.

WHOOSH

DRAW LINES FROM A POINT OUTSIDE YOUR DRAWING TO INDICATE SPEED LINES.

DON'T BE AFRAID TO ERASE IF YOU FEEL THAT YOUR BASIC SHAPES SHOULD BE CHANGED.

EAGLE

A SIMPLE BUILDING SKYLINE AND A
LARGE CLOUD HOLD THIS TOGETHER.

THE FINAL BASIC SHAPES YOU SHOULD DRAW LIGHTLY
IN PENCIL, IN STEP THREE, ARE THE WINGS.

CAPTAIN JOG

A DIFFERENT TYPE OF JOGGER... HE JOGS ON TOP OF TALL BUILDINGS.

STEP 1-

STEP 2-

STEP 3-

STEP 4-

YOU SHOULD DRAW BOXES FOR THE BASIC SHAPES OF THE BUILDINGS AFTER YOU'VE COMPLETED STEP FOUR OF THE FIGURE.

SIMPLE LINES
MAKE A GRASS
TEXTURE FOR
HIM TO STAND
ON.

KEEP THOSE HAND SHAPES LARGE SO THAT HE CAN REACH
AND CATCH THE BALL.

EAT·TOO·MUCH

VARIOUS PEN AND INK
PATTERNS WERE USED
TO COMPLETE THIS —
NO SOLID BLACKS
WERE USED.

LIGHT
SOURCE

PATTERNS USED

KEEP THE BASIC SHAPES LARGE AND SIMPLE.

EVIL DR. X

USE A SERIES OF
SHORT LINES TO DRAW THE
GROUND SHADOW AREA.

DRAW THE BASIC SHAPES OF THE FIGURE FIRST BEFORE
PUTTING CLOTHES, CAPE OR HAT ON HIM .... IF YOU DO ....
HE CAN GET VERY NASTY !!

SPACE FIGHTER

... COMES DIRECTLY FROM *PLANET-Y* TO THE PAGES OF THIS BOOK.

A SILHOUETTE OF THE CITY SKYLINE AND A FEW STARS IN THE SKY ADD INTEREST.

STEP 1-

STEP 2-

STEP 3-

STEP 4-

YOU CAN EXAGGERATE ANY OF ITS FEATURES...
IT WON'T MIND TOO MUCH.

CRIME STOPPER

A COMBINATION OF PEN AND INK PATTERNS AND BLACKS WAS USED IN THIS SCENE.

COMPLETE THE BASIC SHAPES ON THE HERO FIRST BEFORE
CONTINUING ON TO THE VILLAIN.

ALTHOUGH THERE ARE MANY AREAS
OF BLACK IN THIS SCENE – THEY
HAVE ALL BEEN HANDLED VERY SIMPLY.

NOTE THAT THE BASIC SHAPES OF ONE FIGURE HAVE
BEEN COMPLETED BEFORE THE OTHER.

KNOCK-OUT PUNCH!

THE SIMPLE
BACKGROUND
SUGGESTS THAT
THIS IS AN
OUTDOOR
SCENE.

BY KEEPING THE SMALL AMOUNT OF BLACK ON OUR HERO
ONLY, HE STANDS OUT FROM THE VILLAIN.

STEP 1-

STEP 2-

STEP 3-

STEP 4-

AFTER YOU'VE DRAWN THE BASIC SHAPES OF OUR HERO-
DRAW THE BASIC SHAPES OF THE VILLAIN THROUGH THE OTHER
SHAPES. THIS IS THE ONLY WAY TO DRAW HIS SHAPES
CORRECTLY.

TWO WITH ONE BLOW!

BECAUSE THIS IS A COMPLICATED
SITUATION – THE BLACK AREAS
HAVE BEEN SCATTERED
IN A SIMPLE MANNER
BETWEEN THE HERO
AND THE VILLAINS.

STEP 1–

STEP 2–

STEP 3–

STEP 4–

MASKED HERO

KEEP THE BLACK
AREAS ON THE
HORSE AND
RIDER ONLY.

LIGHT
SOURCE

ADD DUST

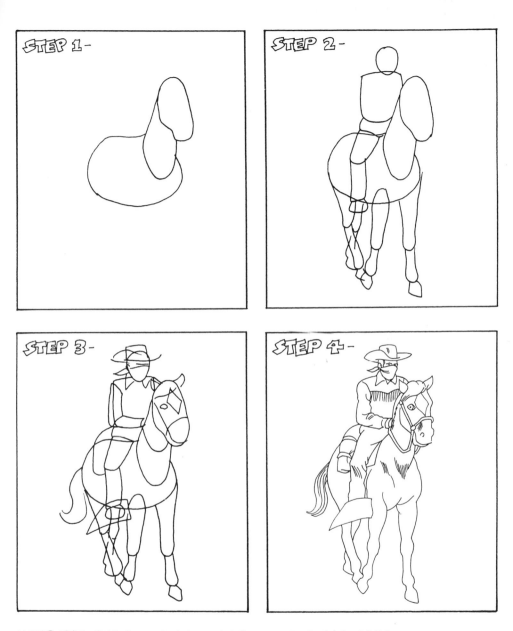

KEEP THE SHAPES SIMPLE AND FOLLOW THE THREE
PRELIMINARY STEPS TO YOUR FINISHED LINE DRAWING.
ADD SHADOWS AND BLACKS ONLY WHEN YOU FEEL THAT
YOUR DRAWING IS READY.

HERO HORSE

A SIMPLE GROUND LINE HOLDS THE HORSE IN POSITION.

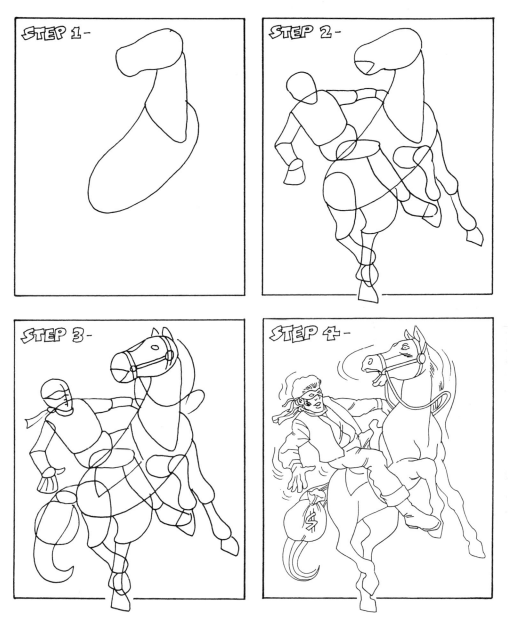

THIS IS A VERY COMPLICATED DRAWING— BUT, JUST AS THE
OTHERS— START OFF WITH SIMPLE BASIC SHAPES AND
ADD OTHERS TO THEM LIGHTLY IN PENCIL.

SERGEANT SKETCH'S COMICS

NOW THAT YOU'VE LEARNED TO DRAW THESE CHARACTERS, HELP ME COMPLETE THIS STORY BY DRAWING THE MISSING PICTURES. START BY DRAWING ME!

DRAW SERGEANT SKETCH FROM PAGE 10 HERE.

IT WAS A QUIET STAR-FILLED NIGHT WHEN THE CITY OF METRO WAS VISITED BY THE EVIL SPACE FIGHTER FROM PLANET-Y!

SOON METRO WILL BE SWARMING WITH MY ALLIES... AND THE CITY WILL BE MINE!

DRAW SPACE FIGHTER FROM PAGE 44.

FORTUNATELY THE EAGLE WAS ON WATCH.

THAT LOOKS LIKE TROUBLE!

DRAW EAGLE FROM PAGE 34.

BEFORE HE COULD MAKE A MOVE, EAGLE WAS SURROUNDED BY EVILDOERS!

I SURE COULD USE SOME HELPFUL FRIENDS RIGHT ABOUT NOW.

DRAW THE EVIL DR.X
FROM PAGE 42.

DRAW EAGLE
FROM PAGE 34.

DRAW THE EVIL DOME-
HEAD FROM PAGE 24.

EAGLE WAS OUTNUMBERED...BUT NOT FOR LONG!

HANG ON BUDDY,
HERE WE COME!

THE SPACE FIGHTER'S GANG ARE NO MATCH FOR US!

DRAW CHECKERS
FROM PAGE 26.

DRAW LEAPING LINDA
FROM PAGE 28.

SOON METRO WAS CRAWLING WITH CRIME STOPPERS.

THERE'S NO ROOM FOR THE LIKES OF YOU IN THIS CITY!

DRAW CRIME STOPPER AND THE VILLAIN FROM PAGE 46.

IT WAS A NIGHT THE GOOD PEOPLE OF METRO WOULD NOT SOON FORGET.

SOMEONE COULD GET HURT WITH A KNIFE LIKE THAT!

DRAW KARATE KICK SCENE FROM PAGE 48.

I'M GETTING OUT OF THIS PLANET!

USUALLY WHEN THE LEADER FALLS... THE REST FOLLOW!

DRAW SPACE FIGHTER FROM PAGE 44.

DRAW SPEED QUEEN FROM PAGE 18.

SPEED QUEEN WAS RIGHT, SPACE FIGHTER AND HIS GROUP FLED METRO AND OUR PLANET, NEVER TO RETURN.

THANKS FOR HELPING ME TELL THIS STORY!

DRAW SERGEANT SKETCH FROM ONE OF THE FIGURES ON PAGE 10.

PIRATE PETE

DO YOU HAVE ICE CREAM?

SIMPLE WOOD TEXTURE

THIS IS A BRIDGE DRAWING BETWEEN A REALISTIC AND A CARTOON FIGURE.

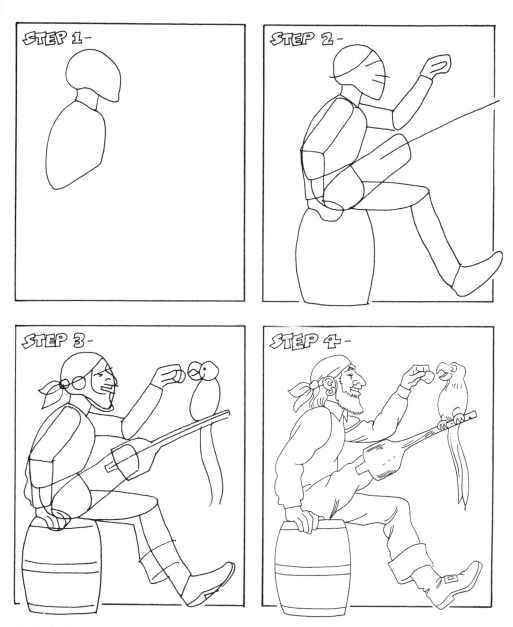

DRAW THE SHAPES OF THE PIRATE FIRST BEFORE DRAWING
THE SHAPES OF THE PARROT.

WACKY FOOTBALL ☆

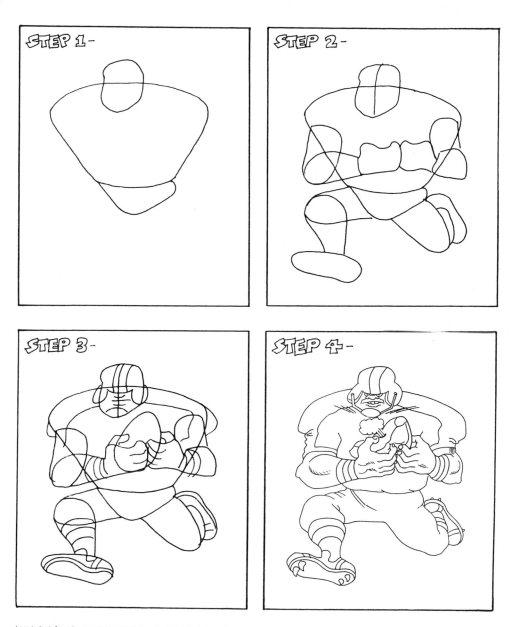

WHETHER DRAWING A REALISTIC OR CARTOON FIGURE, THE
PROCESS IS THE SAME. DRAW THE SHAPES AS SHOWN IN
STEPS ONE, TWO, AND THREE — AND THEN COMPLETE YOUR
LINE DRAWING AS IN STEP FOUR.

LIM-BURGER RAT

YOU DRAW AN ANIMAL CARTOON JUST LIKE YOU'D DRAW
ANYTHING ELSE. START WITH THE BASIC SHAPES
AND BUILD ON THEM.

SHOW-BIZ DOG

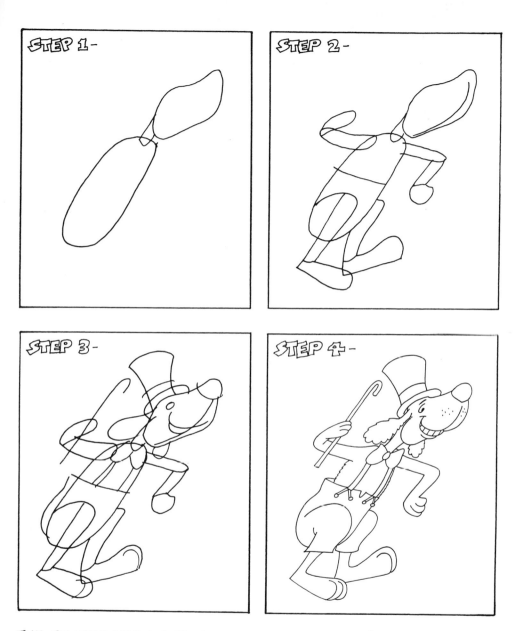

THE SHAPES LOOK STRANGE – BUT, DRAW THEM LIGHTLY IN PENCIL AND BUILD ON THEM.

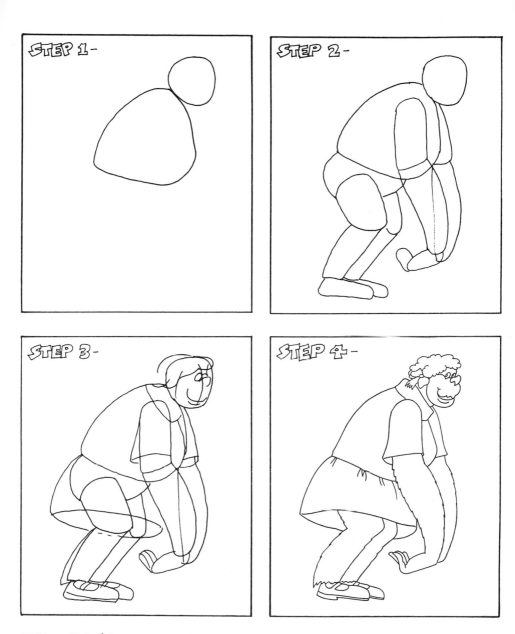

IF YOU DON'T DRAW THE BASIC SHAPES OF HER LOWER
BODY— YOU WOULD BE GUESSING AS TO WHERE THE LEGS
CAME OUT OF THE SKIRT IN THE FINISHED LINE DRAWING.

CAVEGUY CALVIN

DRAW THE RIGHT ARM AND HAND SHAPES FIRST, THEN
ADD THE CLUB SHAPE.

WHATA WITCH

THE HUMOR COMES ACROSS BETTER IF YOU DRAW AN
ENVIRONMENT OF SKY AND BUILDINGS.

DRAW THE ARM AND HAND SHAPES BEFORE DRAWING THE
BROOM SHAPES- THEN ADD THE WHEEL SHAPES. ADD THE
HAT SHAPE TO THE HEAD-MAKING SURE IT FITS PROPERLY
ON THE HEAD SHAPE.

COOL BEAR

THE SPEED LINES SHOW
THE DIRECTION THAT THE
SOUND IS COMING FROM.

DESIGN YOUR
OWN "COOL"
TIE DESIGN.

IF YOU DREW
THE MUSIC
NOTE PROPERLY—

IT WOULD NOT
ADD HUMOR
TO THIS SITUATION.
DRAW IT WITH
WAVY LINES.

DRAW THE ARM AND HAND SHAPES BEFORE DRAWING THE
RADIO SHAPES.

ULTIMATE WARRIOR

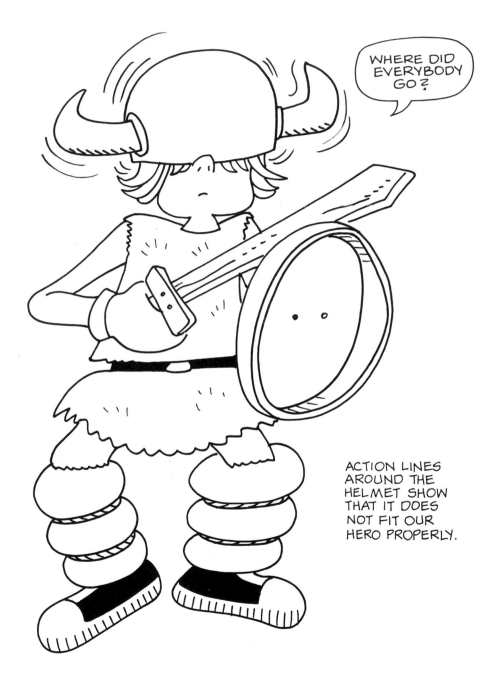

DRAW THE HELMET SHAPE LARGER THAN THE HEAD SHAPE
SO THAT THE HELMET IS BLOCKING HIS VISION.

COMPLETE THE BASIC SHAPES OF THE FIGURE BEFORE
DRAWING THE SHAPES OF THE ROCKET SHIP AND LADDER.

TRICYCLE·KID

THE SURPRISED SUN
AND CLOUD SHAPES SHOW
THAT THE RIDER IS
OFF THE GROUND.

↑ ADD SPEED
LINES AND A
← DUST CLOUD.

DRAW THE HANDLEBAR SHAPES HIGHER THAN THE
HAND AND FIGURE SHAPES.

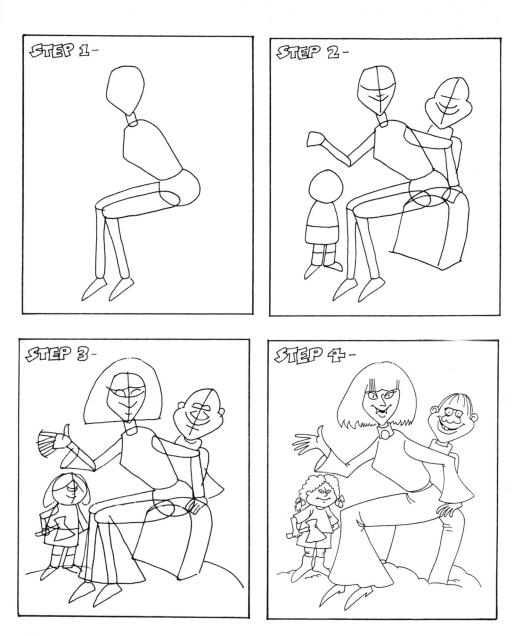

THIS MULTIPLE FIGURE SITUATION LOOKS COMPLICATED —
BUT, JUST TAKE ONE STEP AT A TIME AND YOU WILL DRAW IT.

TRY WRITING AND DRAWING YOUR OWN *"NITRO AND KNUCKLEHEAD"*
COMIC STRIPS LIKE THE ONE ABOVE.
MAKE IT SILLY AND HAVE FUN DOING IT.

THESE ARE SIMPLE CHARACTERS TO DRAW.
DRAW THEM WEARING DIFFERENT CLOTHING.

THE FIGURE OF THE GIRL IS SMALLER BECAUSE SHE IS
A DISTANCE AWAY FROM THE BOY.

THE OFF THEIR ROCKERS BAND

THIS RECORD BREAKING GROUP- (*ALL THEIR RECORDS HAVE BEEN SMASHED*) CAN PERFORM ESPECIALLY FOR YOU. DRAW THEM ON SCHOOL POSTERS, BOOK COVERS, GREETING CARDS AND ANYWHERE ELSE.

JUST TAKE IT STEP-BY-STEP. THIS IS A DIFFICULT SCENE BUT YOU CAN DO IT! JUST CAREFULLY FOLLOW THESE STEPS.

COMICS FOR FUN

NOW THAT YOU'VE LEARNED TO DRAW THESE CARTOON
CHARACTERS—HERE ARE SOME JOKES TO DRAW THEM IN.
MAKE COPIES OF THESE PAGES SO AS NOT TO DRAW IN THIS BOOK.

THE AIR IS ESPECIALLY CLEAN TO BREATHE ON HALLOWEEN BECAUSE I'M SWEEPING THE SKY THEN!

DRAW WHATA WITCH FROM PAGE 74.

I WONDER IF KING ARTHUR GOT STARTED THIS WAY?

DRAW THE ULTIMATE WARRIOR FROM PAGE 78.

THERE'S NO SPACE LIKE HOME!

DRAW SPACK...SPACE KID FROM PAGE 80.

THE ONLY THING BIGGER THAN A TYRANNOSAURUS IS ITS APPETITE!

DRAW CAVEGUY CALVIN FROM PAGE 72.

I MAY NOT KNOW HOW TO PLAY MUSIC, BUT I SURE CAN CARRY A TUNE!

DRAW COOL BEAR FROM PAGE 76.

I ONCE DATED KING KONG!

DRAW GORILLA-MY-DREAMS FROM PAGE 70.

DID YOU HEAR THE JOKE ABOUT THE LIMBURGER CHEESE? NEVER MIND .... IT STINKS!

DRAW LIM-BURGER RAT FROM PAGE 66.

DOGS DON'T HAVE FLEAS... THEY HAVE PUPPIES.

DRAW SHOW-BIZ DOG FROM PAGE 68.

TO AVOID A FLAT TIRE... WATCH OUT FOR THE FORK IN THE ROAD!

DRAW TRICYCLE-KID FROM PAGE 82.

MY TEACHER HAS A READING PROBLEM. SHE CAN'T READ MY WRITING!

MY TEACHER FLUNKED ME IN EVERY SUBJECT... EVEN RECESS!

DRAW NITRO AND KNUCKLEHEAD FROM PAGE 86.

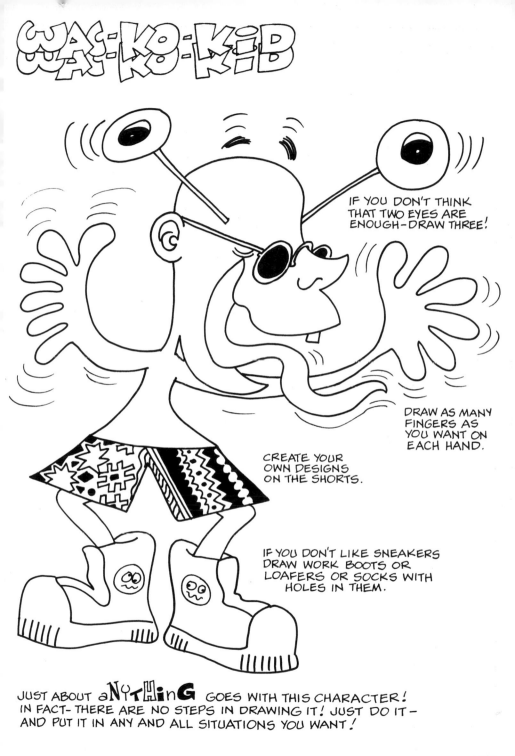